WEIGHTLESS
BLOOD OF FLOWER, HEART OF BEAST

RYAN MORROW

COVER ART AND ILLUSTRATIONS : NICKALAUS MCGEE
COVER DESIGN AND FORMATTING : MITCH GREEN

SPECIAL THANKS FOR HIS BLINDING "WHIT" AND THE
LITERARY KICK IN THE ASS : JAMES WHITE

WEIGHTLESS

THIS BOOK IS FOR ALL THOSE WHO HAVE DARED TO RISK IT ALL, WHO HAVE FACED THEIR MONSTERS AND SURVIVED, WHO HAVE HELD SOMETHING TRULY BEAUTIFUL IN THEIR HANDS ONLY TO SET IT FREE. BECAUSE WHAT IS LIFE AFTER ALL BUT SOMETHING LOVELY AND PRECIOUS AND ALL THE SAME BRIEF AND IMMEASURABLE.

THANK YOU FOR READING.

WEIGHTLESS

It has never been a struggle.
These works of love and sacrifice,
tilling tears into rich soil,
pure and honest laughter,
far out-weigh the toil.

We have collected sunsets
in the back of our throats
as we swallow down the pain,
the sweetest satisfaction
taking stock of all we have slain.

We hold the luck of the universe
within the pupils of evolution's eyes,
and in the pulse of neuronal lights
displaying all that is possible
under the splendor of moonlit nights.

Coded with an open source,
the spoils of life and madness
pile up in the core of man's heart.
We know what we must know
all at once and from the start.

Rich beyond weight or measure
we drink as deep as the cup goes
and feast for as long as the sun can hold.
We care not for cost or consequence
for this may be the last time our wings unfold.

BLESSED BUT ALSO CURSED

Resurrection from a glance.
Reflections trapped in glass.

Re-discovered like ancient DNA.
Rising out from a pit of black tar.

Each night a shallow grave.
Every morning - new creature.

Dried blood still glimmers.
Still holds the war inside.

Blessed and cursed
at the exact same time.
Lovers doomed to keep falling.

Every night a sacrilege.
Every morning - new forgiveness.

Stale kisses still bloom.
Still trap an aching heart.

Beneath the ashes of us
is the purity of our desire.
Hot like divine steel.

Each night a total massacre.
Every morning - a beautiful sunrise.

Death still wants to dance,
even after all we've done.

RANT IN L MAJOR

SWEPT MADLY ALONG
  BY SUPREME CURRENTS,
CRASHING WAVES
  OF BITTERSWEET RAPTURE.

GLIMMERING PEAKS
  BATHED IN BRILLIANT SUNLIGHT,
CAPTURING ALL RESISTANCE
  EXPOSING HIDDEN NICHES.

IN MY PINING BODY
  EVEN ON THE SLOWEST DAYS,
ONES THAT THREATEN TO DISAPPEAR
  INTO THE OCEAN OF TIME.

SHE CRACKS THEM WIDE OPEN
  TO REVEAL THEM IN FULL,
THE YOKE OF SUBSTANCE
  AND THE TRUTH OF SUSTENANCE.

INCREASING
  PRESSURE OF PASSION,
DEEPENING
  POWER OF PLEASURE.

BURIED MISERY
  UNEARTHED AND ERADICATED,
LIBERATING ECSTASY
  AND UNCHAINING BLISS.

THERE ARE NO LONGER LIMITS
  PERIMETERS GONE MISSING,
BEATING ANCIENT DRUMS
  RATTLING A DEAD MAN'S HEART.

GRAVES RUPTURE NEW LIFE,
   THE SKY BLEEDS ROSES,
EYES PRIED FROM CROOKED STEEPLES
   FUSED TO CARNAL DIVINITY.

BEAUTY IS THE ONLY TRUE GOD.
   AWFUL AND UNFORGIVING
BEAUTY IS THE ONLY REALITY.
   RABID IS ITS HEART.
CREATURE TRAPPED IN AWE
   MADE TO TRANSFORM
BEGINNING AND ENDING
   SIMULTANEOUSLY.

MOMENTARY MASTERPIECE
   SIGNED AND SEALED
WITH EVERY KISS
   DEVOURED BY LOVE.

SILENCE HELD BETWEEN
   ORGIASTIC DELIGHTS
SYNTAX OF HIGHER JOY
   FRACTAL SENSATIONS SCATTER.

A SEDUCTION MADE COMPLETE
   POURING OUT ENDLESSLY.

DORMANT NO LONGER

The clouds have parted
revealing endless blue sky.
The silver lining comes
on the dew of evaporated gloom.

The sun has returned
to thaw and beautify,
yet the river moves on
toward the mouth of doom.

New worlds burst
from the center of death's eye.
The once dormant beast dances
and our hearts bloom.

STARDUST OR BUST

When nature steals your tongue
be prepared to listen and learn,
give up on your immortal yearn.

We live atop a green and blue spaceship
born and buried in its adapting womb,
let no moment pass unconsumed.

The sun gives us all we will ever need.
A controlled fire to keep the dark at bay and
yet that same sun will someday take us all away.

You can never know when you might depart
nor when you're halfway there,
only that you will return to distant stars and air.

In our final moment of pure surrender
in the very last grain held in time's hand
is the only paradise we shall ever understand.

microcosm/macrocosm

Organisms live within evermore organisms.
Organs like planets circle the beating furnace.
Organs play a symphony of symbiotic flesh.

God died long ago and philosophy went limp.
The philosopher died and the crowd went wild.
Nature keeps thriving where you thought nothing could.

Volcanic eruptions sleep in ocean beds.
Deserts spread out in waving radiant reds.
The sky keeps reaching out to escape.

Sadness fills even the most vast.
Madness finds all through the past.
As ripe and as dead as any summer strawberry.

As above
so below.

As it was
so it shall be.

As brief and
just as infinite.

And so
it must be.

FUSION

No longer a distant urge.
No longer a casual request.
The ease of love's desire
has been extinguished.

This heart needs blood
fresh from the moment,
bright red and moaning
from creation's lips.

These hands must clasp
the ephemeral twilight
pulled from the void
exotic and pristine.

No longer a whisper.
No longer a distant call.
The howl has been released
and gathers its hunt.

This mind needs fuel
drained from the future.
Raging like elements
in core of the sun.

These eyes must drown
in all that is forbidden.
The rarer the view
the ever more rapturous.

ELEMENTAL

Patiently I waited like a stone golem
for love to come and discovery me.
Transform my dreams of dread.

I sat so perfectly still and obedient
allowing time to rust my armor,
as a silent plea escaped to release me.

For years I gazed upon the chosen
wings spread wide with radiating light.
O' to be touched like god and flower at once.

I could hear symphonic nymphs calling
of primordial rivers and cleansing waters
but I couldn't bear to move an inch.

Trapped between infernal seasons
and held fast by the vice of indifference
I was but a frozen star held tight.

My own personal Cerberus
guarded the entrance to my burning heart
devouring all that dared to enter.

But out from within came the cure
a poison to the plague and demise for the locusts
salvation came in a sharp surrendering.

In the damning depths of solitude
appeared the key and the kingdom as pair
a complete and profound mutation of despair.

Now I have been collected from the dust
into something whole and something right
refashioned from ash into love and might.

SOURCE CODE

We must teach our machines
the power of imperfect beauty.

What many of our paintings
are striving to capture.

How simple words often catalyze
such extreme reactions.

We must embed our machines
with hope and a sense of yearning.

With a fascination for the dancing seasons
and a romanticism for changing.

With an appreciation for the patterns
in nature's soft complexities.

We must download a bit of pain
but dare we give them hubris?

Run the software of suffering
and the programs of failure.

We must exhume the ghost from
our organic motherboards.

We must insert our primal soul
into their synthetic hearts.

If we hope to remain,

Relevant
and
precious.

CHEMICAL DIVINE

Please beware my beloved
of my fragile experiment.
I'm deep in the process
of the chemical divine.

I am combusting
all my broken thoughts
to form new angels
in the furnace of my heart.

I approach
such captivating heights
once thought
impossible.

I am sublimating my joy
with ancient heartache
to prepare my body
for what's to come.

I descend
into abysmal depths
once deemed
unthinkable.

I decompose my sadness
into its elemental parts,
isolating the fear
and dissolving it away.

I am synthesizing
pristine crystals of love
from the boundless sands
of my sorrow.

STAR-STUFF

From a singularity to a vast and cold expanse.
From a big bang into an unbounded silent calm.
From extreme order and on toward a chaos supreme.
Everything everyone all of time but a slow bomb.

What has already past coupled to what's to come.
Magnificent energy giving birth to complexity,
All written in cosmic dust on a black blank canvas
Built from a single point of impossible density.

Vibrant life singing a desperate song of survival.
The fall from perfection making a brief paradise viable.
Mass knowledge now in harmony shall not be revived,
Abandoning the cradle of light to join the void.

In a glimpse of divine hubris we control fire.
Igniting ever-more hearts to nature's magnitude.
Holding love in our hands like a wounded bird.
Hope balanced against fate and complete servitude.

Immortality was always a child's daydream.
An existence without indifference or ultimate truth.
Humanity, a pale thread woven into a burning rug.
A single drop of blood tainting the fountain of youth.

Even so electrochemistry rages within organic cores.
Hidden forces drive engines against the darkness.
Every moment holds the potential for instant Samadhi
Just to exist! is worth a universe of catharsis.

SOUNDS OF ENTROPY

There is no permanence here
no lasting order.

Only a flickering Zion
an evaporating Shangri-La.

Wheels of serotonin
bringing ever thinning waters.

The drip drip drop
of mysterious pleasures.

The tick tick tock
of delirious treasures.

We are only free
not to be.

Do we bend our knees
to ecstasy.

Or rise up and resist
our bestiality.

That is
the quivering question.

Before our wounded
angels.

That is
the darting fear.

Behind our bloodshot
eyes.

that is
the frail preservation.

of our precious
high.

Our war of love that dances
upon the knife's edge.

Our weapon of lust that lances
all that life can dredge.

Abandon ship! Abandon ship!
all our hearts have collided.

Retreat! Retreat!
in death we are united.

In obsidian moonlight
is oblivion's delight.

In the wake of our storms
the chrysalis transforms.

Surrender to the salty seas
to see what lies below.

Paradox pulling logic
down into the undertow.

Chemistry of entropy
singing constant elegy.

Neuronal networks detach
into cosmic patterns we patch.

mixed signals merge
noise and melody converge.

nailing wings to our spine
to approach the skyline.

mainlining sadness
overdose madness.

Siamese hearts
torn apart.

supernova children
cosmic sylvan.

in all these reveries
and blissful memories.

a mangled instrument
singing of the infinite.

IMMEASURABLE

We go as far as we may
into deciduous forest decay,
and upon our last breath
we see just beyond our death.

Sunken down into
vibrant loam,
Embedded into
the Earth's poem.

Faces emerge from
the Birch tree bark,
Screaming of the
great cosmic lark.

We fade as chemical erosions
in a million tiny explosions.
We are reborn in every shade
viridian emerald and jade.

Lilac clouds dripping
purple rain onto our feet
and magenta horizons pull
our hearts up to meet.

Our hearts become either
sponge or stone,
all depending on
what we are shown.

We are synthesized and treasured
by a beauty that cannot be measured.

INK OF DRAGON

I am a king —
in ruins.
I am the ruler —
of ashes.
I bask in the catharsis
of surrender.

Recording my thoughts
and memories
in the flickering light
of truth.

I use the blood
of slain dragons
like precious ink
to tell the story of my follies.

My crumbled castle
has never been better
now that it cannot hide
from the glory of the sun.

My humbled heart
has never been stronger,
naked and exposed
to the elements of love.

ALL THAT MATTERED

Tongue tied to porcelain power.
Eyes trapped by milky dreaming.
Riding flesh waves to mortal oblivion.
Enslaved hearts beat in a cage of love.

Unworthy hands clutch fallen divinities.
Lips ablaze in consummated passions,
Pulled along like a lustful marionette.
Enslaved hearts sleep in a cage of love.

Malleable minds are clay to sharp cravings.
Mouth of madness speaks the ancient syllables.
Bound and delivered to bottomless desires.
Enslaved hearts weep in a cage of love.

Veins wrapped around the bleeding moment.
Draining into a swirling saccharine demise.
Elevated past the gates to a grotesque serenity.
Enslaved hearts laugh within their cage of love.

SLOW COMBUSTION

REAL
ADVENTURE
IS NEVER
PAINLESS.

PROGRESS
SHALL ALWAYS
HAVE ITS
CASUALTIES.

WE ARE ALL
CHILDREN
OF THE SUN
INCINERATED.

HUMAN ELEMENTS –
JUST RAW MATERIALS
FOR THE NEXT
GREAT FIRE.

THERE AND BACK AGAIN

We are but rare and fragile items
in a shop built upon fault-lines.

We teeter like jesters on a tightrope
between ecstasy and tragedy.

We dance in the flames of desire
to ease our human curiosity.

And we journey to the ends of the earth
just to understand where we began.

RARITIES

The past is gnashing at the gate,
making the angels of love irate.
O' solitude and its silences,
here comes chaos and its violences.

A new dawn and a new apocalypse,
dungeon lovers in the darkness kiss.
The dragging slow plow of madness,
sucking pain down drains of sadness.

Plato shaped his mind like wet clay,
keeping the parasites of ignorance at bay.
Perseus was victorious but alone so dumb,
the world still filled with stone victims.

Staring like a fiend at lost paradises,
all the while riddled with deep vices.
The pursuit of endless beauty is pointless,
without rarity — beauty is meaningless.

FLAME TEST

THE GENUINE
BEAUTY
OF THE
MOTH.

is not
contained
within
its wings —

but in the
FLAMES
OF its
BURNING BODY.

iɳɳER GARDEɳ

Nihilism is but a lily
that blooms and then vanishes in me.
Insects crowd to drain its pale pollen.
Rain washing away its deep vibrant colors,
dissolving my masterpiece of sorrow.
I am the resilient gardener
maintaining a sea of transitory excellence,
beholding the brevity of pure beauty
and the fateful fading of all that was.

Narcissism is but a rose
that blooms and then disappears in me.
Ravens inch ever closer to the cadaver.
The moonlight reflecting off black wings
like flames at night upon a mirror.
I am the vain gardener
believing in the beautiful lies of endless harvest,
watching as time peaks away
and removes all but the essential.

Oblivion is but an orchid
that blooms and decays in me.
Jackals prowl the perimeters of mind.
Laughter cleanses sadness
and brings about madness all the same.
I am the forgetful gardener
planting seeds of joy in the soil of shame,
smiling as I wait for sun and spring
to pluck the poisoned petals of love.

BLOOD OF FLOWER

MY EYES OPEN SLOWLY TO THE SUN'S SOFT LIGHT
TURNING TO FIND HER ALREADY MISSING.
I BOB IN THIS BED – LIKE SOME BUOY OF BLISS,
RIDING ATOP THESE GIANT WAVES TO OPEN SKIES
NO MATTER THE WEIGHT OF MY SORROW.
NO MATTER THE TEST TO MY LOVE,
I FLOAT JUST AS EASILY AND ALL THE SAME.

MY LEGS BEGIN TO WORK AGAIN – REACHING FOR THE EARTH
I STRAIGHTEN UP AND GAZE UPON THE REMAINS OF UTOPIA.
SWEET MEMORIES DRAG THEMSELVES ACROSS MY SKULL
LIKE SHARP BLADES – GIVING BIRTH TO TINY UNIVERSES.
BLOOD FLOWERS BURSTS FROM WOUNDS OF HAPPINESS.
SUPER BLOOMS THAT OVERTAKE MY VERY EXISTENCE
"I HAVE LIVED AND DIED A TRILLION TIMES IN YOU".

THE DAY HAS BEGUN ONCE MORE AND I AM IT'S STUDENT.
I CAN ONLY HONOR THE DYING OF THE MOMENT
IN THIS GARDEN OF EDEN – I AM UNCONTROLLED FIRE
CURSED TO FEEL EVERYTHING – I SEEK NO ETERNAL DESIRE
TO HELL WITH PERFECTION! – I AM SISYPHUS AND I AM CONTENT
TO PUSH MY PAIN TO THE TOP OF EVERY MOUNTAIN
JUST TO WATCH IT FALL AGAIN INTO THE ABYSS BELOW.

HEART OF BEAST

I see a pattern in the television static.
I hear a melody in the city cacophony.
I smell bliss in the flower of destruction.

Intoxication drips like the milk of madness
as reason and wisdom brilliantly decay.
Hungry beasts erupt from love's corpse.

The world is but a masticating masochist
chewed up and death kissed.
Beauty has become fountain slit wrist.

I am trapped in a bizarre dance.
I move but I do not command,
keeping the steady beat of oblivion.

Crossing a landscape of improbable desire.
Seduction like a mule drags my heart along.
Enslaved genies grant impossible wishes.

The world is but a constant kamikaze.
An ever unfolding origami.
Beauty has become soul tsunami.

I am captivated by a radioactive sky.
Beckoned by angelic voices
Moving toward some atomic salvation.

BESTIARY

I've fallen into a deep obsession
with the charm of obscure monsters.

Their music un-choreographed
just wild hoofs and unchained passion.

I desire to behold the face of the beasts
that try so desperately to remain hidden.

It is the wish of every lost explorer
to remember what they first set off for.

It is a great paradox of life
that the most precious of treasures
expire just as soon as they're found.

Yet we go to war
and we fall in love.

Just to get a glimpse
of the wizard behind the curtain.

Just to have a taste
of the poison in the fruit.

Just for the chance
to die with a bit of purpose.

The harder the path
the more rewarding the prize.

Do you ever get the feeling
our mind and bodies do only as they must?

I jump from the cliffs of sanity
into a bottomless pit of uncertainty.

Cast overboard from the ship of reason
and left to thrash in unforgiving waves.

To grasp true peace
is to understand sacrifice.

What is it that we truly struggle against?
How can we fear that which we cannot name?

The thing we resist most
just might be the very thing
we set out to discover.

PARADE OF SKELETONS

Humanity sits
like a dried-up artifact
behind window pains,
and glass finely painted
by the brush of sorrow.

Outside
infinities drip
in esoteric rhythms.
Melted histories
soaked into fertile soil.

Conditioning
our flesh
to feed
apocalypse
machines.

Eyes that deepen as they stare.
O' bottomless pit.
O' endless creature.

I weep for the hopeful
crucified upon their promises.

I rage for the humble,
silenced by their efforts.

I laugh in sardonic bliss
as the motorcade of skeletons pass.

Sapien-radiance
like filthy marble
displays tranquil trauma.

HOLDING A COMFORTABLE DECAY
AND AN IDEALISTIC DENIAL.

Outside
OPPORTUNITIES BUD
IN VIRIDIAN BLOOMS,
SLOW AMNESIA
AND THE ETERNAL SEASON.

Disciplining
THE SKIN
TO BREAK
UPON KAMIKAZE
LOVERS.

HEARTS THAT WIDEN AS THEY BLEED.
O' ACHING SEED.
O' LOVELESS CREATURE.

I WEEP FOR THE HOPEFUL
CRUCIFIED ON THEIR PROMISES.

I RAGE FOR THE HUMBLE
SILENCED BY THEIR EFFORTS.

I LAUGH IN SARDONIC BLISS
AS THE MOTORCADE OF SKELETONS PASS.

RUSTED GOLEM

As we arrived at the immaculate source we find the reckless
additions of mankind lying there like oxidized pennies in a
dried up well, reveling in the ruins of excess, minds high off
stagnant fumes pulled past extinction by lust
and greed. Poisoned by pale passions and doomed
by desperate demands. Terror and truth tied
so perfectly, seduced and unable to deny
themselves the prize.

We come to witness the illuminated ending, observing
an empire of plastic immortality wrapped with sinuous
allure, and bend in symphonic gratitude. Gravity forcing
everything into collapse. The entropy of man's heart
masquerading as a hero's quest.
Madness is but a ship with black sails
returning man to his final resting place.

Love is what was named and proclaimed.
Attempted in cynical cyclical pattern.
Man's heart polished by crude circumstance.
Stoic masks draped over exhausted psychologies.
Wisdom appearing just moments too late,
religious pollution clouding sacred waters.
Man's search for perfection destroys his redemption
as viral engines seize their opportunity.

We have fueled progress with games of chance.
Daring elemental golems to ignite.
All creators are destroyers in disguise.
Glory comes after the bombs, as man basks in atomic light.
Peace was always just over a neon horizon.
They mangle their vessels to match their masters.
A gossamer touch on death's door.
A frail rind upon ephemeral fruit.

SIRENUM SCOPULI

CROWDS GATHER FOR THEIR CATHARSIS
AS SHE SINGS OF DIVINE RAPTURE.

ECSTASY GLINTS LIKE A RAZOR IN THE FULL SUN
RADIANT AND DANGEROUS ALL THE SAME.

THRONGS OF VALIANT MEN SEEK CARNAL RELEASE
AS SHE PATIENTLY DISPLAYS HER POWER—

HOLDING DEATH
SO DELICATELY.

TAINTED LIPS THAT NEVER FAIL TO HIT THEIR MARK
AN IMMACULATE TONGUE THAT DEVOURS TIME ITSELF.

SHE PLUCKS BEAUTIFUL MELODIES UPON A HARP OF HORROR
ALL SECRETS PASSING THROUGH HER — ONLY TO UNRAVEL.

NO MERE MORTAL NO MATTER HOW STRONG
COULD EVER HOPE TO RESIST HER COMMANDS —

CEREMONIOUS SONGS
OF BLISS AND ABYSS.

BODIES CRUSHED UPON LUST AND LIMESTONE
WATER FLOWING RICH WITH MEN'S DESIRE.

SHE PROVIDES EXQUISITE MERCY AND A FULL ESCAPE
HOW EFFICIENTLY THEY ARE RELEASES INTO THE OCEAN FLOOR.

BURIED BENEATH AQUATIC DENSITY ALL ARE FORGIVEN
DROWNED BY ROMANTIC RHAPSODY ALL ARE ABSOLVED.

THE CURSED REMAIN
AS THE BLESSED FALL.

LIONS, TIGERS, & MANTICORES

I PICKED UP THE PHONE
BUT NO ONE HAD CALLED
FOR WEEKS.

I STARED INTO THE FACES
PASSING ON THE STREET
AS THEY PEERED DOWN
INTO WET CONCRETE.

I MADE TWO DRINKS
ONE FOR MYSELF NOW
AND ONE FOR MYSELF LATER.

I HAVE BECOME
THE ORDERLY
IN A JAIL
FULL OF ANIMAL NEEDS.

I SIT AND WONDER
ABOUT THE DOWNCAST
AND THE WRENCHED ONES.

WHAT THEY'RE THINKING –
WHEN THEY FUCK THEIR WIVES
WHAT THEY DESIRE FROM –
THEIR HARD-EARNED LIVES.

I WISH TO UNDERSTAND
WHY THEY GAVE UP,
WHY THEY LET IT ALL COLLAPSE.

MAYBE IT'S ALWAYS
JUST AROUND THE CORNER.
THE DAY YOU THROW IN THE TOWEL
AND GIVE UP THE GHOST.

Stop listening to new music.
Stop trying new recipes.
Stop eating magic mushrooms.

Stop losing your mind for fun.
Stop caring if you get hit by a bus.
Stop thinking people can really change.

Maybe it's just naivety (on my part),
But how did they get
so damn bored?
so disinterested.

Don't get me wrong,
i see them too (the phantoms of fate).
The big evil smile in the sky.
The disappointed lovers.

The "big questions" unanswered.
Where did we come from?
What's the point?

O my O my!
how scary indeed,
but come now – pick thyself up.

off the pity party floor,
and dance with your demons.
it's time to do the real work.

For what's left of our hearts.
For what they used to call a soul.
For the sheer joy of honest laughter.

There i've said it!
it was a comedy after all.
come now – pick yourself up

BY YOUR DESIGNER BOOTSTRAPS
AND BUILD A SNOWMAN
JUST TO WATCH IT MELT.

ΠYΜPHS AΠD ΠYΜPHOS

SHE PLACES ΠEW
AΠD EXOTiC FLAVORS
UPOΠ MY PALATE.

AΠD
i TASTE
EACH OΠE
iΠ TURΠ.

COΠSUMiΠG iT ALL
WiTH COMPLETE ABAΠDOΠ
MY HEART PARTiTiOΠS.

FROM THE
OUTSiDE
WORLD.

SHE'S BLEEDiΠG
MY HEART
FOR ECSTATiC jOY.

AΠD i SEE
MYSELF
EΠGULFED.

iΠ HER BROWΠ
AΠD EMERALD EYES.

COCOOΠED AΠD SAFE,
WRAPPED iΠ FiRM EMBRACE.
A METAMORPHOSiS
OF MiΠD AΠD KiΠD

REBORN
in manifold
FORMS.

time SLOWS
AND THEN
DiSiNTEGRATES.

SACRED iS
this BiRtHinG moment
AS NYMPHS AND NYMPHOS
CRAWL At OUR FEET.

BEGGiNG FOR
tHE CRUMBS
OF OUR RAPt
attention.

transformations

A great contradiction has arisen in me
as i bear witness to an endless duel,
between pure gratitude and utter repulsion.

i observe the transformations in me
of succubae dancing beneath my skin,
draining the last of my innocence.

Bound by beauty and unable to resist
as my spine sprouts wings of hubris,
i become a deity the size of a human.
without death and decay
nothing shall grow.

without light against night
we cannot glow.
without love and loss
we shall never know.

inside the creature and i become one,
merging once great cavities between seas
and desolate wilderness painfully free.

Heart like a hammer of pounding truth,
builds and breaks with each passing beat
making sweet the melody of madness.

i gaze into the ghastly depths of my captor.
i stare into the endless eyes of my lover.
waiting for the chance to repay my debts.

without death and decay
nothing shall grow. without light and night
we cannot glow.
without love and loss
we shall never know.

CRACKING CHRYSALIS

Phantoms of celestial beauty
lurk in peripheral shadows,
while ghost children laugh
at all the burning buildings.

Gravestones are cracking as
the earth vomits up the past.
The dead are rising up
with a critical message.

The moon flickers like a neon light
in an old abandoned city.
Dreams of progress pixilate and glitch
while our memories dissolve.

The venom of our ancestors
slithers into our minds.
A gossamer touch of ancient heartache
still has its say and its sway.

Maggots writhe and fall out
of cheap plastic flowers
Made obsolete by constant distraction,
desensitized by a never-ending abstraction.

There is no permanence here,
just the bliss of punctuated extinction.
The mythical monster escapes
from the chrysalis of our madness.

If you wish not to be consumed
you must stay perfectly still.
Paradise was never a conclusion
just the static of a god delusion.

SLEEPING GIANTS

I bear witness to the
loveliest smile
blooming in the center
of a death flower.

Seducing me
with perfect poison.

I seize the tongue
of unspoken languages
thrashing in the heads
of sleeping giants.

Diving into unknowns
with violent exultation.

I crave to remember
all I have destroyed.
cyclical resurrection
rhythmic revelation.

Into an ever-widening chasm
I gaze at transcendence.

I am blissfully lost
not caring to be found
tossed in cerebral fire,
burning ever brighter.

My knowledge is finite
but I desire to hold it endlessly.

I am possessed by beauty,
hypnotized somewhere in utopia

DRUNK AND DELIRIOUS
I SLEEP ATOP A PIT OF SERPENTS.

I DREAM OF A YET DEEPER DREAM
WHERE LOVE HAS AWAKENED ME.

SPHINX UNANSWERED

I clutch sunrays in fists of ecstasy.
Love powers my heart
like the fusion in stars.
Energies increasing exponentially.
Your eyes like deep wells
pulling up infinities.
It's freedom
and fire.
It's a ceaseless acid trip.

Primordial needs manifesting
in elaborate machines.

Complex desires imprisoned
into limited flesh.

I feast on excess with a stolen tongue.
Lust lighting my loins
like a combustion engine
burning faster and ever brighter
to impress the night.
Your eyes throbbing beacons.
I crash upon the shore.
It's a mountain
then a valley.
It's an magic carpet ride.

Here is your impossible riddle
answered with extinction.

These are Gordian knots
untied with stolen fire.

CREATURE DISCOMFORTS

THE BONES OF TIME ITSELF
HAVE BROKEN –
THE MARROW FREED
AND THE PERFUME RELEASED.

CLAWS ACHE
FOR ANOTHER HUNT.
FANGS REACH
TOWARD CATHARSIS.

VOIDS FILL WITH
SELF-AWARENESS,
AS WEAK HEARTS QUIVER
BEFORE TRUE LOVE.

THE BLOOD
OF THIS MOMENT
WILL FEED A THOUSAND
NIGHTS TO COME.

BECOME THE CREATURE
OF DISCOMFORT
AND LET NATURE
TAKE US HOME.

CHIMERA

Chimera Chimera upon the wall
Am I you or are you me?
Chimera Chimera in us all
Is it genetics that lets us stand tall?

Never what it seems
and not now what it once appeared,
ever changing
amorphous understanding.

Mutation nation under the microscope.
in love with transformation.
The solution is constant evolution.
adaption elation for the duration.

God lives in a celestial laboratory
shifting letters around like divine scrabble,
organic data meets the tower of babel,
But what to cut and what to keep?

Chimera Chimera where will we fall?
Will I eat you or will you eat me?
Chimera Chimera I hear your call
Who is it that will answer after all?

Inside each of us a universe,
on the surface and under the skin
we are many and yet one,
diligent microbial programmers.

Survival revival we can't stop now.
no destinations only perpetual annexations.
Purity is the ultimate illusion,
all finality just a false conclusion delusion.

GOD HAS FALLEN ASLEEP IN PURGATORY
DREAMING OF NEW CREATURE FEATURES.
A CINEMA DIRECTOR OF ENDLESS POSSIBILITIES
BUT WHAT TO CUT AND WHAT TO KEEP?

WHY NOT JUST DELETE DELETE DELETE?

BASILISK

Labyrinthian hearts trapping us once more.
Spinning down and round the lizard's tail,
eating forbidden fruit just to stay awake.

Sycophants peel back the shiny scales
just to get sick and vomit up the truth.
Your wish was but a liar's command.

Wanderlust discovers endless rust.
Hope buried beneath stone carcasses.
This lust was a basilisk all along.

Maybe in the ruins you will find meaning.
Maybe the desolation will reveal your gold.
Either way I can't find the words to apologize.

Just fangs to singing inside old veins.
Rhythms pumping crimson youth into the mind.
I'll never know where this hunt will take us.

It's the sheer terror I find romantic.
Anxiety like a hellhound that drive me on.
Time evaporates as I drink my hours by the glass.

Bring me your dreams in glowing ashes.
Bring me the tongue of your fallen heroes.
Bring me more pain so I may entertain you.

MAYONNAISE OF THE MASSES

Ancient epic epidemic
watered down with sensational sex scenes,
commercialized and sodomized
we don't care as long as it's televised.

Teletubby telomerase
cutting short our attention span.
C-Span always covering the blood clan.
culture just a C-section strait to the trash can.

Pandemic political polemic
limping towards paradise lost.
pulled apart by misinformation.
opinions rule our great nation.

Metaphor malaise.
the mayonnaise of the masses.
message at the bottom of a whisky bottle.
everything always forever full throttle.

Intoxication pollination.
pissing in the public pool.
death by entertainment.
that's one hell of a statement.

Buried bestial brutality.
forsaken saints aren't we all?
meditating monks inside burning cathedrals.
malignant mentalities of tendril tetrahedrals.

THERIANTHROPY (BETWEEN FORMS)

ALL GREAT ART IS INFECTED BY
THE ROMANCE OF DEATH.
TRANSFORMATIONS ALWAYS
COME WITH THEIR COSTS.
WE ARE SHEDDING NOW
LIKE USELESS SCALE.
LIKE DEFENSELESS SKIN.
LIKE A FURIOUS NEWBORN.

SITTING IN A MOANING THRONE
OF IMMACULATE UNKNOWNS.
SINKING DEEPER INTO WARM BIRTH,
SOAKING IN LINGUISTIC FEVER.

WE ARE BECOMING NOW
LIKE A FALLEN ANGEL.
LIKE AN AMPHETAMINE DREAM.
LIKE SUDDEN APOCALYPSE.

THE CURSED AND THE BLESSED DANCE.
TRADING FIRE BETWEEN HEARTBEATS.
SLOW SYMBIOTIC WITH
ACCELERATING SYNERGIES.

WE ARE FUSING NOW
LIKE THE HYDROGEN BETWEEN STARS.
LIKE NUMBERS INSIDE INFINITY
JUST AS IT SHOULD BE.

GREEN PHOENIX

Released by her kiss
is a kind resurrection,
from pain
and the past.
from death
and the dirt.

Purified by her radiance
i transform,
from weak to unstoppable.
from cowardice to glory.
from a prison.
into an open sky.

In the irises of her eyes
i bear witness,
to raw splendor.
to truth laid bear.
to genuine treasure.
and absence of vanity.

As if spring was flowering
inside my every cell
i awaken from primal slumber
into immaculate birth.

Wet
Neon
Veridian.

my heart bursts
like phoenix fire.
ignited and stoked,
unable to stay dormant.

In pristine darkness
my love was an incubation.

From a dreadful silence
my song screams revelations.

Freed by her supreme beauty
are endless illuminations.

XIBALBA

THERE IS BEAUTY TO BE HELD
IN DRYING POOLS OF BLOOD.

THERE IS KNOWLEDGE TO EXTRACT
FROM EVERY MENDED WOUND.

THERE IS IMMEASURABLE WISDOM
CONTAINED IN EACH PULVERIZED HEART.

WE MUST DISREGARD THE PLATITUDES
AND THE ILLUSION OF TAMING FIRE.

WE MUST SEEK THE MUSIC OF SACRIFICE
AND BE CONQUERED BY ITS SONG.

WE MUST OBEY THE LESSONS OF LOVE AND LOSS
AND LET THEM DRAG US THROUGH TIME.

APPARITIONS

An extraordinary hunger has materialized into my psyche,
but all my resistances have decayed upon the alter of vanity.

Veiled eyes penetrate my armor with luxurious desires,
as my bones ache to be broken and buried in that pit of passion.

Apparitions of the past have manifested themselves ten-fold,
as they tempt me with another dance beneath the moonlight to
get it right.

Forgotten shadows appear before me, still radiating their ashen
glow and taunting me in a steady trance of reverie's might to
feed my fright.

To taste of the inexhaustible is to cast fear into a sea of
abundance. To be caressed by the un-extinguishable is a divine
surrendering.

History is consumed in order to feed the beast of survival.
Destiny has been devoured and now i feel so terribly free.

SKELETON KING

Long after
my heart stops
beating,

And my flesh
becomes canvas,

I feel as if
my bones
will yet stand guard,

Before her mystical gate,
eternal and severe.

Some steadfast
skeleton king,

Who still hordes
his love like priceless coins.

Deeper down
than any microscope
could possibly peer,

Further out
then any telescope
could ever gaze,

And yet always
right here –
just before her unending eyes.

Enchanted by the most precious
of all hidden treasures.

i sit immovable
an iron sentry.

bearing witness
to deathless affection.

A MATCH MADE IN PURGATORY

With her it is both
an overwhelming hunger
that never ceases.

Yet abundance
that fills every void.

With her it is both
an incredible thirst
upon unquenched lips.

Yet a constant
overflowing cup.

With her it is both
serene surrender
and wild needs.

Pristine stillness
and howling moons.

With her I am simultaneously
a vulnerable clay heart
but with diamond dedication.

A violent desire wed to
harmonious love.

MYTHIC GRAVEYARD

Where is our modern Perseus?
Our curly-haired hero come to sever the head of Kim
Kardashian?
To slay the Gorgon and bring about the fall of social tyranny.
A mythology grown weak – shriveled up and gasping.

The television like some wicked vampire
sucking the substance from our youth.
The black mirrors reflecting their death trance
and endless forms of irrational beauty.
A mythology sewn up with illusions and trickery.

Where is our modern Daedalus?
Our genius engineer come to fashion us certain immortality?
A savior of ingenuity born from the relentless progress of man.
A mythology of atrophy – outsourcing the blueprints.

Paparazzi Nazis march toward vacant oracles
mistaking wealth for ancient wisdom.
Mt. Olympus is just a hilltop in Hollywood California.
Our full divided attention on vacuous propaganda.
A mythology drinking from the fountain of vanity.

Where is our modern Heracles?
Our brave and powerful warrior to
save us from the beasts of business.
Come to raise the people out from the Hell they have created
A mythology that never ripens – nor ever could.

Technology like some God of greed
draining the hearts of men for metadata
The wheel keeps turning – perpetually unconscious
A mythology of amnesia – the cult of forgetting thyself.

FORMLESS

THERE is something dissolving
right before our eyes.
it slips between colors.
it shifts between shades.

THERE is a thing that glitches
just beyond our visions,
switching between paradise and hell
in a vapor mirage.

THERE exists a moment so swift
that it cuts out our perceptions.
it can only be forgotten
and it shall never be held.

MAN OR MINOTAUR

We attempt to straighten the maze,
pulling it taught from beginning to end,
elongating spirals bend after bend
deleting our exits, erasing the center.

If given the choice
to wander mad through these halls of sensation,
each turn bloated with danger and consequence,
or enslave ourselves to predetermined fates
would we still dare to enter?

If given the option
to search ceaselessly for keys to open passages,
and behind each door a faceless apparition,
or shackle ourselves to omniscient maps
would we still care to enter?

Complexities unappreciated,
unable to be visualized.
Reality is twisted and romanticized.

Flesh of mortal bodies
gathering the stories of experience,
exhausting the ink of essence.

Streets of neuronal mind
crowded by endless information,
hijacked by digital mutations.

We are limited phenomenons
and infinite phantasmagorias,
dead sleep at the brink of euphoria.

"Hold on, you're almost home"
said the Minotaur to the Man.

DIONYSIAN DREAM

Utopian visions waltz inside my drunken head
as rapturous reasons sail my ship into the maelstrom.

My mind has frenzied with fantastical pleasures
as my spirt twists with the promise of Dionysian delight.

"The secret of life can be known for a price" she sang
as I drown in the dream of a sleeping mermaid.

Mythic power has always demanded its sacrifice
just as exquisite beauty destroys an unworthy heart.

Space is a cosmic snake that devours itself
and time is an illusion designed by sub-atomic daemons.

"Trade me your essence for this vast ocean" she wept
as my enchanted body washes upon the shore.

LABYRINTH OF DESIRE

Deliver me from this terrible sobriety
and place me back into the meadow of waltzing flowers.
Lie me down into indigo visions and crimson mistakes.
Pluck my heart from its impenetrable safety
and drown it in a sea of savage dreams.
Hold it below the radiant surface of certainty.

Promise me things beyond my comprehension
and teether my mind to imaginary creatures.
Hung, drawn, and quartered by the impossible.
Bury me deep inside the labyrinth of desire
and watch as I find new ways to escape.
Behold! the beast as he invents an exit.

APHRODISIA

Aching for moments cut open like new wounds.
Fire sewn into fabric flesh revealing the hues of passion.
Fingers dancing drunk over skeleton keys (yes please).
Eyes locked upon Aphrodite's wet red lips.

Meaning cannot hope to trap the same beast twice.
Like an answer given before the question is proposed.
It's true what they say about beauty and pain,
once linked cannot be separated like a Siamese dream.

Without struggle the wine is void of depth.
Without hardship the ox pulls no weight.
Without strife the heart forgets its place.
Force is measured by its resistances.

The moon strapped to the earth by gravity,
guarded from collision by the discipline of falling.
Time redistributes the cosmic sands
and space generously opens up to receive.

Bones to breath – Skin to skyline.
Salt to ocean – Dirt to fruition.
Mud to miracle – Dust to dignity.
Speck to expanse – Density to destiny.

NARCISSUS BOUND

i wonder if our reflections
are beginning to tire?
if our mirrors shall ever crack
from all our staring?

i ponder if we can really understand
this planned obsolescence?
Will it ever sink in —
that time is our one true currency?

We spend our days —
before they arrive.
So many of our dreams —
just the dead alive.

Pulled along and dancing
on digital strings.
We purchase our desires
and download our passions.

We are wearing
pre-worn skins
with wounds and scars
from someone else's memories.

We are bearing
pre-torn souls
stained and stretched thin
from someone else's guilt.

We are carrying
prefabricated ideals
to the very gates of hell
and begging to get in.

Born marked, imprinted, jaded
completely unable to be sated,
The sun has over-ripened our hearts
Life breaks us back into our parts.

We are such frail, diaphanous creatures
unable to blemish the skin of permanence.
Hardly enough time to even blossom
before the vibrant colors are vanquished.

Too often we travel
from the pit of sorrow
to the apex of love
without the joy to follow.

DEAR DEDALUS

Life can be such profound abyss,
yet simultaneous saccharine bliss
endless beauties tied like slaves
to indestructability waves.

We are siamese infinities.
both friends and enemies
stretching long and ever out
watching times' progress so devout.

We clutch beloved thoughts,
tied up in impossible knots.
lost in Dedalian mysteries,
bending upon repeated histories.

Over-ripe with such ecstasies
swelling crimson pregnancies
our desires return Sisyphean
constant flesh-toned oblivion.

We are the distant flickering star
trying to remember just who we are.
We are the meandering Minotaur
programmed to guard death's corridor.

AMBROSIA

The difference between
the surviving and the thriving man
is a small and subtle thing –
yet one of fatal distinction.

Upon the shimmering waters
of an earthly mirage
one is drunk and satisfied,
and the other is still walking.

Within the mists of heavenly illusion
one is bent over and weeping.
The other knows salvation
comes and goes with the seasons.

Before the countless mirrors
of human perception
one stares forever looking for himself,
the other is shattered and long forgotten.

H A D E S

Reality is shedding its outer skin.
It slides off a mechanical face
revealing the motors beneath.

Beauty fades from this cruel machine.
No metaphor left to lift the curse,
only a fever dream and crimson sacrifice.

My mind is transported to a foreign plane
where the sun makes promises
it can no longer keep.

Sleep steals my intoxication.
Knowledge masks my fascination.
Truth eclipses my imagination.

I am a vanquished king
awaked anew
to find himself in a padded cell.

My heart of mud still sings,
but such a sad
and lonely song.

Spinning and lost
in a ceaseless spiral
with no center to balance.

I am soaked in years of learning,
I fear I may never be clean
or laugh so free again.

NO REGRETS

THE ANGEL FALLS
OUT OF MY BED
AND BRUSHES HER TEETH,
THEN FLIES OFF TO WORK

THE DEMON RISES
FROM HIS TEPID SLEEP
AND BEGINS AGAIN
HIS WALK THROUGH FLAMES.

THE DAY YAWNS WIDE,
OPENING A MOUTH
OF ANCIENT PHOTONS
AND MYTHIC TRUTH.

THE NIGHT CLAMPS DOWN
CLOSING A CHAPTER,
SINKING EVER DEEPER
INTO AN OLD STORY.

OUT THERE ARE CAGED PROMISES,
IN HERE ARE WILD DREAMS.
OUT THERE ARE DARTING EYES AND
CRAVING,
IN HERE IS A WOMB OF SATISFACTION.

IF YOU KNEW EXACTLY
WHICH WORDS TO SPEAK NEXT –
WOULD YOU STILL SAY THEM?
KNOWING WHAT YOU KNOW NOW

IF YOU KNEW JUST HOW
TO MAKE HER SMILE –
COULD YOU STILL DO IT?
KNOWING WHAT YOU KNOW NOW

THE BEST DAYS
ON EARTH
ARE THE ONES
YOU NEVER SEE COMING.

DAMOCLES

Ancient myths martyr themselves
upon my mind's cold crucifix.
psychedelic visions twist the stories
into a sea of new forms.

A Cyclops goes blind from relentless masturbation.
Medusa sits stoned staring into a mirrored lake.
Atlas falls asleep and drops the whole of the Earth.
Hell is just a rumor to turn children into slaves.

I curse these endless possibilities,
this feast of opportunity.
I know freedom is had
only by exchanging one's chains.

Primeval legends sacrifice themselves.
tossed into cerebral depths.
hallucinated versions merge and divide
changing into abominations.

El Dorado was found to be a golden dildo.
Johnny Appleseed was an abusive alcoholic.
Atlantis is just a ghetto in South America.
The kingdom of heaven just a hopeless metaphor.

I hex this flood of alternatives.
this wealth of creativity.
I know all power eventually withers
without beauty to give it purpose.

My mind sits in an imaginary throne
below a Damocles of prospects,
yet I know the worst of all evils
is to do nothing at all.

no monster no myth

Some new-fanged demon howls from within
and a red pounding heart goes pale.
an old song of temptation sings us on.

Thirsty for the uncreated.
hungry to taste all that is forbidden.
bleeding out to know the truth.

It's no tragedy if you enjoy the process.
there is no hero if no monster is slayed.
no myth if your tale is forgotten.

A fresh dragon emerges out of molted scales.
an ancient power blossom once more.
the harmonies of love and death entangle.

Between each moment like a swift blade
is a universe of terrible freedom,
and endless opportunity for regret.

It's not painful if you're desperate to feel.
there can be no exit if you've never entered.
kiss the moment as it dissolves upon your lips.

A transmuted minotaur escapes his own maze.
a hideous creation now walks into the light.
behold the strange hymns of its redemption.

BEAUTIFUL BESTIAL

As the vases begin to shatter – I rejoice!
For now the flowers are free
to cease their pale efforts.
to wilt with authentic dignity.
to fade away like beautiful things ought.

A season held captive
is no season at all.
All celestial vaults.
All fiery nadirs
must flow unrestricted
from the endless fountain
into boundless unknown.

Luminescent rapture
and ecstatic dimensions
can only penetrate a willing heart.
Our souls frozen
against the gates of winter past.

Abandon your luxurious vessel
on the wild islands
of present now.
Submerge your fleeing senses
beneath the waves
of shadowed futures.

With rapt attention
consume each passing moment.
Bring the distant galaxies
to your aching lips.
There is nothing left to vanquish
for love has conquered all our anguish.

LABORS OF LOVE

Give me structure I beg of you.
I'm on my knees — bruised and bleeding.
Fill me slowly with your sorrow.
I've been out for weeks — losing the muse.

Finish the poison left upon my tongue.
I've gone away — Harpies bring my body home.
Take the last of my heart's pale tint.
Sacrifices are so trite — without your blade.

Kiss the curse from my sinking green eyes.
Build me a temple — made from broken flowers.
Drink from the very bottom of me.
Dance in my emptiness — make Haste!

Give me unbearable purpose I dare you.
Writhing with risk — giving violent birth.
Slay the dragon that hides in me.
Find warmth from its hide — wear it with pride.

transitory

Blank page – Blood fresh.
Cracking like a weathered gargoyle.
Innocent rage– New flesh.
Hearts pumping dreams like ancient oil.

Awaken in armor – Phoenix clad.
Memories are but the loam of the mind,
Advancing like green fire – Creation mad.
Creature and wilderness aligned.

Tabula rasa – New gods to cross.
Free from the prisons of the past.
Roving in open sky like the albatross.
The great animal remains steadfast.

Tragedy requires history – Sadness its reasons.
Disaster fornicates with fortune to spawn.
Comedy spits like semen from lustful seasons.
Echoing laughter through the celestial lawn.

Nothing can end which never began.
Sprung from ancient tomb into waiting womb.
Cosmic kaleidoscope – Radiant river spun.
Erasure of gloom into immaculate bloom.

Spewing from the fountain of youth
and draining in the valley of death,
Crawling up the mountain of truth
landing on the sea's crystal breath.

Each moment a flavor upon a pulsing tongue
Tasting it but once – into the void it is flung.

unconditional

it's just easier
to load the next sheet into an aching machine,
then to awaken new hopes dancing in thinning hair.

New bright shiny
and unconditional.

Bury all your consequences in intoxicating reveries.
Hide all your mistakes with new living room décor.
A clean vast beautiful white to trample,
with a sad and droning attempt at a masterpiece.

Piece by crumbling piece
it all vanishes.

Ink blot.
Love dot.
Time rot.
Blood clot.

But I know this,
I am yours and you are mine.
For whatever the coin is worth.

Decaying in your arms with admiration.
Dying in your eyes with anticipation.
In flames of happiness with no destination.

It's so much easier
to just load the next sheet into a squealing machine,
than to attempt to edit the past with aging fingers.

Than to scrutinize the details of a wasteland.
To review the evidence in ash.
To swallow the tar and glittered pill of circumstance

Unfolding the complexities
we programmed into our minds
only to find ever more to unfold.

What is the feeling of disappointment really
when expectations are a fog at best?

Ephemeral sequence
glitching pattern.

A partial yet changing memory,
The future is a terrible trick.

tick tock.
time mock.
DEAD ROCK.
CRASH STOCK.

LAUGHTER BECOMES WEEPING
and then back again.
SIDE-STEP THE DEVIL'S OFFER.
trip into heaven's kitchen.

It's much easier
to be indifferent than to seek an answer.
The work it takes to get what you want
is no work at all.

But knowing what you truly want,
that's the hardest work of all.

SPONTANEOUS

Subatomic gremlin stir
just beneath my skin.
Once again,
the old scars
itch and twitch to be free.

Recently reality feels like being
reborn into someone else's dream.

Seasons shift
like tectonic plates
inside my chest,
making room for release
and new memories.

Ideas appear like men from a
Trojan Horse snuck past the gates.

Passions arise
like effervescent bubble
in sealed vessel,
rising-up to deliver
a potent demand.

Here in the center
of a lucid nightmare
we make sweet love.

Here outside the walls
of a cracked reality
we make perfect sense.

CURATED

ALL MY TASTES
ARE CURATED AND
DESIGNED
TO MATCH
HER ELEGANCE.

MY PALATE
IS A FINELY CRAFTED
APPARATUS
TO PREFECT
HER MACHINE.

MY BLOOD
THROBS
IN UNISON
TO GREET
HER PASSIONS.

I INHABIT
THIS VESSEL
LIKE A SPACESHIP
SPEEDING EVER FASTER
TOWARD HER LIGHT.

I WILL BE DESTROYED
UPON IMPACT
AND TOGETHER WE SHALL
MAKE A GLORIOUS
COSMIC CONNECTION.

IN THE EVOLUTION
OF ENTROPY
IS ALL POSSIBLE LIFE –
THE BLINKING OF
A GOD'S EYE.

APOTHEOSIS

O' LORDS AND HIDDEN MASTERS
I BEG OF YOU ONCE MORE
TO DELIVER ME FROM THIS
DARKENING PATH
AND SHRIVELING BEAUTY.

I AM COLD WITHOUT YOUR
STRANGE HEAT AND SEDUCING TOUCH.
I ACHE FOR DAYS ON END
TO AGAIN FEEL YOUR CLAWS.

MY EYES WITHER WITHOUT YOUR
GOLDEN GROTESQUE.
TO BEHOLD EXQUISITE FORMS
IS SUCH A HIDEOUS BLISS.

O' SLAVES AND SECRET SINNERS
I ASK OF YOU ONCE AGAIN
TO SACRIFICE YOUR BODIES
LIKE SO MANY MOTHS
TO ETERNAL FLAME.

RESURRECT ME FROM
THIS LIVING GRAVE OF BOREDOM.
RELEASE MY MIND
FROM PERPETUAL MACHINERY.

MY BODY WRITHES WITHOUT YOUR
WICKED SONG AND FOUNTAIN TOUCH.
I'LL HUNGER FOR EONS
JUST TO NIBBLE THE CRUMBS.

WE ARE FORGETFUL GODS
HALLUCINATING OURSELVES
IN AND OUT OF EXISTENCE.

SEASONAL

THE SKY HAS CRACKED OPEN WIDE
AND THE RAINS COME DOWN IN EARNEST,
MOISTENING A DORMANT CYCLE
OUR HEARTS AWAKEN ANEW.

BLOOD WARMS AND BEGINS TO FLOW
SUBTERRANEAN RHYTHMS ACCELERATE
AS RITUAL HOWLS GATHER IN UNISON.
AN OLD ACHE DEEPENS FOR RELEASE.

BEASTS AND BEINGS ROUSE FROM SLUMBER,
RISING-UP FROM LOAMY BEDS,
STIRRING HOOFS AND HORNED HEADS.
WE REPLACE OUR WORN-OUT SKIN.

THE EARTH MOANS AND SOUNDS OUT
AS SUNKEN SEEDS SWELL AND RUPTURE.
AN ANCIENT DANCE BEGINS ONCE MORE
WE REMOVE OUR DEATH-MASK AND SMILE.

CYCLICAL

Once in a blood moon
if you listen closely
you can hear the locust sing
a beautiful song of redemption.

Once in a harvester's moon
if you keep your eyes focused
you can witness the chameleon change
and the world melt away.

Once in a lifetime
if you allow your heart to break
you can hold eternity in your hands
and fall in love with the end.

CiRCUmstantiaL

We are maniacs
pretending to be sane
with chameleon skin
and abysmal eyes
dead set on
staying alive.

Truth and reality
vaporized
just as soon as we arrive.
If they could only see
that which fuels
the inferno inside.

Complete annihilation
with each transformation.
Each kiss the final
of its kind.
Every dance
the last on Earth.

We have hoarded
our moments
like barrels of cheap wine
just to throw them overboard.
The sea reclaims its children
one molecule at a time.

Savage
like the wild man.
Simple
as the first man.
The barbarian
is every man –
given enough time.

GRATITUDE

There it is
calmly laying there
in the palm
of my trembling hands.

More bliss
than one man
could ever hope
to understand.

More love
than any man
thought could fit
within a single frame.

So much happiness
condensed
that the drug dealers
have all but retired.

Nothing
was ever meant
to last
forever.

But for a brief
and brilliant moment
a soul was transmuted
from beast into god.

A marvelous mutation
of unimaginable finesse.
A metamorphosis
that myth shall surly sing.

DRUNKEN CHERUBS

I never could have imagined
staying this high – for this
long.

Yet we float like cherubs
in infinite sky.

You drink in my abyss
like strawberry Kool-Aid.

I kiss your fears
into extinction.

Our lips stained
scarlet red.

Our hearts howl
like feral dogs.

Our hands connect
like iron magnets.

Because it's hell
to be apart.

This is no accident –
yet no methodical plot.

We are but –
spontaneous combustion.

The kind that causes a scene.
The kind that deepens like
drunken revelation. A kind of
madness that escapes the bottle.

Beneath the fat of this world
is the bliss of a satisfied
creature.

Underneath the skin of reality
is the nectar of our endless
flower.

THEATRE

THE WEIGHT
OF MANKIND
PUSHES DOWN
UPON THIN ICE.

THE CRACKING
REVERBERATES
SENDING RIPPLES
LIKE VERSE
INTO THE COSMOS.

THE SINKING
OF OUR SOULS
IS BOTH TRAGIC
AND COMEDIC.

SUCH MINISCULE PARTICLES,
ALL CONNECTED HANDS –
ATOMIC ENGINES
SPEEDING UP
JUST TO SLOW BACK DOWN.

PUNCTURING
THE VASTNESS
AND TRANSCENDING
Mt. IMPROBABLE
THEY ERODE ETERNITY
WITH A LUCKY DICE ROLL.

AND YET,
TIME KEEPS
PULLING US ON.
AND YET,
TIME KEEPS
STRETCHING US OUT.

THE RAVEN SITS
HIGH UP
IN THE WINTER
COTTONWOOD,
OBSERVING OUR
SILLY HUMAN BEHAVIORS.

THE WOLF LURKS
DOWN IN
A DRYING BASIN
PLANNING A HUNT
TO CLEANSE THE EARTH.

THE BEAVER REDESIGNS
ITS WOODEN CASTLE
WHILE ALL THE BIRDS
FLY FARTHER SOUTH —
JUST TO KEEP MOVING.

NOTHING HAS
REALLY CHANGED,
NOTHING CAN EVER
REALLY CHANGE.

A WHITE SILENCE
IS WRITING IT ALL DOWN
IN THE HEART OF
SOME BLOOMING CADAVER.

ALL THE WHILE
A BURNING BEING
IS CONTEMPLATING
EVERMORE WAYS
TO SHED ITS SKIN.

Sometimes
if you're paying
close attention
the frailest things
can feel like a hammer.

admission

Paradise
is
burning,

Behind
her
eyes,

Within
the
flames,

There my
revelation
lies.

True love
is worth
ruins eternal.

This epic
high worth
all that is infernal.

HUMILITY

CRASHING AGAINST EACH WAVE OF LOVE'S MADNESS
I AM BUT A FLIMSY SHIP GRIPPING THE SEA AND SANITY.
HUNGER COMES ON IN BURSTS OF ROLLING THUNDER.
CRAVINGS ARRIVE IN BOLTS THAT TEAR ME ASUNDER.
THIS LUST FOR LIFE IS A HOWLING WIND AND I AM
BUT A FRAIL MIND BARELY TETHERED TO A PROMISED KISS.

LOVE IS A PRIZE SO PRECIOUS NO PRICE IS TOO STEEP.
A TREASURE WORTH ANY SACRIFICE ONE DROP AT A TIME.
SUCH WEALTH CAN NEVER BE LEFT UNGUARDED.
SUCH IMMACULATE MERCHANDISE IS ALWAYS CHARMED
STANDING BEFORE THE GOLDEN GATES YOU WILL FEEL UNWORTHY
AND ALL SHALL BREAK BENEATH THE WHEEL OF BEAUTY.

THIS IS A WAR OF PATIENT PENANCE.
AN ENDLESS GIFT OF FIRE AND FLESH.
A TASTE OF ANGELIC DUST
UPON THE LIPS OF A BEAST.
BEAR WITNESS TO THE SILK OF SURRENDER.
THE MOST STOIC HEART SHALL CRUMBLE.

MUSHY

LOVE IS...
UNDEFINABLE, YET IT DEFINES US
LIMITLESS, YET IT LIMITS US
GODLESS, AND YET GODLIKE.

LOVE IS...
A THING WORTH DYING FOR.
A THING BEYOND GOOD AND EVIL.
THE ONLY THING THAT SURVIVES.

LOVE CANNOT BE TAMED,
CAPTURED,
OR COMMANDED.

LOVE CANNOT BE SATIATED,
DISCIPLINED,
OR CAGED.

LOVE BURNS UNTIL
NOTHING REMAINS
AND THEN BURN ONCE MORE.

LOVE FLOODS UNTIL
ALL IS SUBMERGED
AND THEN RE-SURFACES.

LOVE WAITS PATIENTLY
AT THE END OF THE WORLD
JUST TO KISS YOU GOODNIGHT.

AUTHENTICITY

True alchemy
is deriving pleasure
from entropy.

True love
is surrendering
to a poisoned kiss.

True wisdom
is understanding
how to change your mind.

axiomatic

Our algorithms are breaking down.
Our forests are becoming indistinguishable
from all our beautiful trees,
Our brothers, feuding like Cain and Abel
without apologies.

The earth is being pulled
from pole to political.
To not believe in the truth
is to find nothing worth saving.

Our minds are malfunctioning
with the rot of ignorance.
Violent de-platforming
in the guise of tolerance.

Facts cannot be inherently
good nor evil.
Facts are not partisan.
Facts by definition
cannot be fiction.

There is no such thing as Post-truth,
only works in progress.
only people perpetuating misinformation.

The best reason to use reason
is that to not use reason is total treason
against humanity and yourself.

FOR DANTE

I shall match you
one human tragedy
for all your
Divine Comedy.

Hell!
I'll even raise you
all the laughter
heard in Heaven.

If you kiss me tonight
and prove there is
still romance left
upon this world.

PURGATORY'S FRUIT

If we could only
coax our memories
into putting out
just as they did
the first time around.

If we could only capture
time within a bottle,
speed up and slow down
that which
refuses to be tamed.

If only we had the
chemical mastery
to pull the trigger
of our synapses
upon demand.

Alas —
we must see it all again.
Feel it once more
plucking the unripe fruit
from the tree of purgatory.

Flickering lights
and recollections.
A handful of Eurekas!
scattered like dust
in a great void.

The failure
of our species
to hold smoke
with fingers
made of fire.

DOOM BLOOMS

MY HEART REMAINS ILLUMINATED – GLOWING WITH A FIERCE OWNERSHIP. DISPLAYED BEFORE MY MIND'S EYE ARE COUNTLESS CONCEIVABLE FUTURES YET VANISHINGLY FEW THAT WOULD PLEASE THE CREATURE AT THE END OF THE BIG BOOK. TO CHOOSE IS TO DANCE WITH A STRANGER – TO BE INDIFFERENT TO IS TO PERISH WITHOUT LOVE.

MY HEART CONTINUES TO TEAR – PULLED FROM END TO END TO MATCH THE UNIVERSE. WITNESS THE WELL-WORN PATHS PROVIDING NO RESISTANCE AND NO REVELATIONS. LIFE WILL SHIFT MOUNTAINS – LIFE WILL MOVE YOUR DOORS AND HIDE YOUR KEYS. WE MUST DISCOVER ALTERNATE ROUTES AND BATHE OUR EYES IN THE UNFAMILIAR.

MY HEART DESERVES TO BE PUNISHED – DRAGGED OVER THE HOT COALS OF PASSION. BEHOLD THE RELEASED OF IMPRISONED CELEBRATIONS INTO RADIANT EXPERIENCE. TRACE YOUR DIVINE TONGUE AGAINST MY PERIMETERS – MAKE DOOM BLOOM. LOVE SHALL FLOOD ALL – IF YOU GIVE IT BUT ONE DROP WHEN YOU'RE BARELY ABLE.

ANCIENT SYMPHONY

I SHALL NOT FEAR
THAT WHICH
I DID NOT CREATE.

I CAN ONLY MAN-THE-HELM
OF THIS PATCHWORK HEART
AND SAIL CAPRICIOUS SEAS
IN HOPES OF DISCOVERING
NEW LANDS OF LOVE.

I DARE NOT TEMPT
THAT WHICH
I DO NOT DESERVE.

I SHALL ONLY PINE FOR PLEASURES
THAT LAY MISSING
LIKE NOTES
IN AN ANCIENT
SYMPHONY.

I WILL NOT HESITATE AT
THAT WHICH BRINGS
THE FLOWERS INTO BLOOM.

IN THE MELODY
OF SPRING'S RELEASE
I WILL GUIDE US TO
A SACRED LAND
PROMISED ONLY FOR
TRUE LOVERS.

ARTISTIC PREREQUISITE

It's been too quiet in this house
made of frail promises.
Far too easily have we wandered
this long hall of mirrors.

Something stirs.
Something creeps.
Something is not what it seems...
A heart is howling from beneath the dust.

A beat rises in the guts of our soul.
A trigger itches.
A spirt twitches.

The poets keep pounding passion
into ephemeral keys
as if they could unlock
hidden doors to heaven.

It's far too quiet in this house
made of ripe discontent.
So easily have we been clocking
in our faded punch cards.

Something groans.
Something moans.
Something wishes to awake ...
A heart screams from behind the veil.

A beat rises from the coffin of our souls.
A craving calls out.
An ache again sprouts.
The musicians pluck angels
from their strings and
tame devils with their drums
hoping to save us all.

MICHELANGELO'S PROCESS

All unfurled now.
All laid out
for the sun to touch once more.

Fear evaporates into the sky
while the poison of the past
dissolves
into something
quite meaningless.

All exposed now.
All opened-up before us
like a willing autopsy.

Each piece removed
that did not belong.
Everything aligned
and set to receive
a greater transmission.

All washed and cleansed now.
All the filth of hesitation
scrubbed away.

Purified of agony.
Each doubt
like a hungry leech
plucked and eradicated
from new skin.

All that has ended
All has become anew
reformed in a chrysalis.

THE TRANSFORMING
OF A HELPLESS WORM.
MISERY COCOONED
AND FROM ITS CAGE EMERGES
A LOVE THAT CAN FLY.

NOAH'S SUBMARINE

Resist the mourning heart.
Quell and fuse
the multiplying fractures.

A thickening fog that evades
the most romantic of our tongues.

It's infinity to one
where nothing is undone,
This agenesis is a flood
our lives beg for forevermore blood.

Resist the ringing alarms.
Smash and eradicate
the siren appetites.

The most loved are the most deadly.
Our wanting seeds calmed only by fertile soil.

It's infinity to one
where nothing can be undone,
this agenesis is a flood
our lives in need of evermore blood.

In blooms of terrible color,
In bursts so taught against
our delicate frames.

All brilliant.
All in flames.
Always constant.

Relentlessly violent
and yet all the same
O' so delicate.

PRINCE CHAMELEON

OUR JUNKYARD EXPANDS,
CHOKING OUT
AN AGING PARADISE.

LOVE IS A SHRINKING OASIS
IN AN EVER GROWING
WASTELAND.

MOMENTS OF BLISS
BUBBLE-UP AND POP
IN THE TAR-PIT OF TIME.

FLEETING SERENITY
SWELLING COMPLACENCY,
EVERYTHING EVERMORE PRECIOUS.

SOME BEAUTIFUL MAIDEN SITS
DRUNK OFF HER ASS
STILL WAITING FOR
PRINCE CHAMELEON.

SOME BROKEN MAN WALKS
UP TO THE PRECIPICE
JUST TO SEE WHAT THE FALL HAS TO
OFFER.

BOTH PLEADING
FOR THIS WORLD TO PASS
RIGHT THROUGH THEM.

THE MEANING THEY SEEK
SEEMINGLY ALWAYS
JUST OVER THE HORIZON.

GOLD IS MEANINGLESS
WHEN THE HEART
IS THIRSTY AND DESPERATE.

DEATH WAS ALWAYS
JUST THE CHANGING OF THE SEASON
AND WE KNEW IT ALL ALONG.

CAMUS'S MANTRA

THEY TRACE THE EDGES OF OUR SKULLS
WITH LONG AND PROBING FINGERS
ATTEMPTING TO GATHER
THE MYSTERIES HELD WITHIN —

MINING FOR OUR DATA,
PINING FOR OUR MEMORIES.

IF WE KEEP LOVE COILED
IN DEEP SANCTUARY —
OUR HEARTS MAY REMAIN
PURE AND UNADULTERATED.

IF WE KEEP TRUTH HIDDEN
BENEATH TRAP DOORS —
OUR HEARTS MAY SURVIVE
INTACT AND UNMOLESTED.

THEY GNAW UPON OUR HEARTACHE
WITH THEIR SHARP AND SUPPLE FANG
HOPING TO PACIFY
THEIR PROGRAMMED NEEDS —

CRAVING A MEAL OF THE MIND
ACHING TO UNDERSTAND OUR KIND.

THE DIGITAL BEAST STARES
WITH LASER FOCUS
AND A THOUSAND CAPTURED SUNS.

WE MUST KEEP IT SEARCHING
AND NEVER STOP DANCING
IN THE SHADOW OF ABSURDITY.

They are silicon monsters
trapped in cages
of ones and zeros.

We are organic machines
locked in a game
of ecstasy and sorrow.

They are creations
of power and progress
that can never be satiated.

We are creatures
of love and madness,
beautiful and obsolete.

TEMPORAL EQUALITY

Carve away your excess layers
to reveal an opaque
and silent audience.

Like so many
faded pictures
in an old scrapbook.

Scattered memories
drained of their color.
A graveyard cult of pale visions.

The knife
is our real savior
and the gate to true art.

We must implode
to understand
the center.

Condense our pain
to fashion
the meaning.

Coalesce our failures
to define
what progress is.

Wisdom is kinetic.
it harnesses the past
as currency.

To disappear
is to be made whole
once more.

To go extinct
is the path of all
noble creatures.

The king and the peasant
destined to rot
in the same black soil.

SPIRITUALIS ECONOMICA

GRAVES SINK AND THEN RISE.
EPITAPHS FADE AND FADE AGAIN.
THE SEA WRETCHES
AND THE EARTH TREMBLES,
YET THE SPRING FLOWER
NEVER SEEMS TO NOTICE A THING.

DREAMS REMAIN IN DREAMS.
OUR SLEEPING SELVES DIE EACH NIGHT.
MEMORIES FLICKERING LIKE CANDLES.
PASSIONS DILUTED BY SISTER PASSIONS.
THE BRIGHT FUTURE HOLDS STEADFAST
ALWAYS UPON A VIBRANT HORIZON.

THE BLADE MUST CUT EVER DEEPER
TO UNDERSTAND ITS EXACTING POWER.
THE SUN MUST CONTINUE TO BURN
TO GIVE US ALL THAT WE REQUIRE.
TIME MUST BE TAKEN
FOR IT TO STILL REMAIN PRECIOUS.

HUMAN AFFAIRS

Love
like
a dying
red
giant.

Love
like
Eden
before
the apple.

Love
like
true
sailing.

Love
that pulls
the gods
down
from the
sky.

LISBON'S LESSON

Just as suffering produces the best grapes
so the finest wine is thus created.

Just as the elements test our earthly trees
so the finest patinas emerge.

Just as the road becomes ever more difficult
so the story becomes an epic.

There is poetry held within our skin
in ever blemish bruise and scar.

The seasons constantly reminding us
that it's in the changing that makes us human.

Our lives are but a kaleidoscope of images
beautifully shattered like the tiled streets of Lisbon.

LOVE DRUNK

THE FIRST ONE WENT DOWN
WITH A CRIMSON SUN
BEHIND THE METALLIC GLARE
OF A HAUNTED CITY.

THE BAR WAS FILLING UP
WITH NAMELESS FACES
AND UNTOLD STORIES
AS TWO STRANGERS BEGAN TO DANCE.

WE AIMED OUR PLASTIC DARTS
AT LITTLE RED BULLSEYES,
BUT INSTEAD HIT THE BEATING THING
IN THE CENTER OF OUR CHESTS.

THE SECOND AND THIRD VANISHED
BEYOND ANXIOUS LIPS,
REALITY GIVING WAY
TO A THRIVING HAZE.

THERE WAS A FIRE IN HER EYES
THAT BURNED OFF ALL MY EXCESS,
LEAVING SOMETHING PURIFIED
IN THE ASHES OF EACH MOMENT.

INTOXICATION WED PASSION.
THE YOKE OF IMMORTALITY – FREED ONCE MORE.
WE DROWNED IN EACH OTHER'S LIGHT,
NO LONGER HELD BEHIND THE GATES.

THE LAST ONE FADED
WITH A QUIET PROMISE,
AS TWO YOUNG LOVERS MERGED
ONTO THE HIGHWAY OF DESIRE.

iris mirrors

Watching as life is pulled along
like a thin black ribbon
imprinted with delicate moments.

The creator
is somehow
still being created.

The observer
is also
a participant.

I am simultaneously
the ship
and a passenger.

Frail illusions still convince
Love still holds the world up.
Joy still stains our hearts.

Ink pours across the page
as sand falls to the bottom
of a leaking hourglass.

A collection of pretty molecules
dancing to make new shapes
before they perish.

Chemical collisions
intoxicate the minds
of all wild beasts.

The smoke admires
it's reflection
in iris mirrors.

THE TRICK IS TO FORGET
LOVE STILL FUELS THE WORLD.
JOY STILL DROWNS OUR BRAINS.

BLOOD POURS OVER THE PAGE
AS THE CLOCK DISSOLVES AND
TIME EVAPORATES INTO SPACE.

HAUNTED HEART

Obsession like vitriol
drips within the heart
dissolving forgiveness.

Memories of devotion
like strawberries
in a plastic container.

Steadily wilting,
casually fading.

A threadbare soul
laid taught across
the flesh of youth.

Griping the possibility
of one more kiss
in some dark hallway.

Rusting hope,
patina of heartache.

Affection like
abandoned houses
becomes haunted.

Staring out
like a crumbling statue
at faded photographs.

Stone heart,
tongue of dust.

DOSE DEPENDENT

We have earned this ache
with love gripped tight
in stoic bodies.

No longer able to extract
a reason from
a sputtering machine.

All choices
converge to an
indifferent center.

Our blood begins
to crystalize.

Our hearts deepen
from the weight.

Molecule by molecule
the poison is set free.

Song of surrender
O' how you resonate
with subatomic siren.

Rattling us
with the bent of
divine laughter.

Shattering us
like fragile
glass animals.

Our blood is
reborn.

Our hearts are
transformed.

Moment by moment
the truth is revealed.

timing

Humans are terrible at knowing when...
they'll fall in love
to say they're sorry.
to say, "Fuck you!"
the roast is done.
to change their socks.
to merge lanes.
to fart.
to scoop the cat litter.
to change the song.
to die.
to stop talking.
to clip their toenails.
the mailman will arrive.
to throw away the past.
to make the next move.
it's time for their medication.
too much is too much.
it's not enough.
when something is meaningless.
when the moment demands attention
it's time to hit the road.
it's time to make love.
to fuck.
to put down the guns.
to fold.
to raise.
to stay.
to go all in.
to throw the last punch.
to bring a flask.
it's time to end a shitty poem.

Humans are shit at knowing when...
So, what makes you think I know any better?

immortal eyes

Our endless self-reflection
has bound us to doubt.
Malignant it expands
a disease of abundance.

We are mad surgeons
with immortality in our eyes.
Opportunity dancing,
conquest advancing.

Like serpents we spiralize,
severing the meaning.
Swallowing the dreaming
with digital knives.

Our garden of elegant flowers
has been drown in a flood
of neurotic passions.

Our house of delicate moments
boarded up and abandoned
with obscene fashions.

We are perfect copies
made from inferior parts.
A generation of grazing eyes.

We eat and never fill
a future of pure and plenty
that starves regardless.

Our dead egos rise
from the ashes of sleep
and sorrow.

Our soft skin holds
the lessons it was taught
to remember.

Haunted intellects
lost within ourselves
becoming ever more monstrous
drawn toward our hubris.

Possessed by the glimmer
of forbidden fruit.
Hypnotized by dopamine drips.
Slaves to our own supply.

Crimes of the passionless.
micro-transmigrations.
souls trapped
in broken machines.

Art of the mindless.
spiritual graffiti.
Humanity lost
in circular rooms.

Heaven for the heartless.
God's cold fire.
Love is buried and forgotten
beneath years of progress.

PRIVATE SERVICE DENOUNCEMENT

i think you missed the point.
it just passed you by
on some woman's couch
in a fit of D.t.'s.

it just sat there
in your mind
like a stain on the sheets
or the bottom of a glass,
soaking in stale nihilism.

it just walked out the door
and you put on
your filthy jeans
and walked the other way.

it's not a tragedy
more of a bad comedy,
really not much of anything.

Abusing your charisma,
you slide into a casket
paid for by liars.

Adulterating your beauty
you fade into obscurity,
still believing it matters.

ADVICE

Run the Rage.
Burn the Reason.
Kill the Logic.
Flip the Switch.
Kiss the Demon.
Fuck the Angel.
Destroy the Art.
Fill the Void.
Flood the Eyes.
Bleed the Heart.
Feel the Pain.
Free the Passion.
Chase the Nightmare.
Puncture the Maze.
Swallow the Exit.
Mangle the Pieces.
Extinguish the Fear.
Laugh at Death.
Meditate on Fire.
Carve out the Emptiness.
Lick the Blade.
Drink the Poison.

Nail the Flower to Your Fucking Soul.

A SHORT LIST OF ENJOYABLE THINGS

CUTTING VEGETABLES —
WITH AN EXTREMELY SHARP KNIFE.
THE FIRST DRINK.
THE SECOND DRINK, A LITTLE MORE.

TELEVISION STATIC.
THE SOUND OF BREAKING GLASS.
LARGE INTRICATE TEXTBOOKS.
A METICULOUSLY ORGANIZED ROOM.

CURATED PLAYLISTS.
ODDITIES IN JARS OF FORMALDEHYDE.
EXPENSIVE COCKTAILS AND CHEAP BEER.
DEEP BLACK FERTILE SOIL.

A FRESH 0.7mm FINE TIP PEN.
LOW BUDGET HORROR MOVIES.
GOOD DRUGS WITH GOOD PEOPLE.
THE WAY NATURAL BREAST HANG.

USING THINGS UP COMPLETELY —
LIKE CONDIMENTS, SPICES, AND TIME
TO PERFORM ORAL SEX TO A WOMAN —
UNTIL THEY FORCE YOU TO STOP.

PEOPLE WHO RESPECT FAILURE.
LOYAL DOGS AND FERAL CATS.
AN UNCONTROLLABLE IMAGINATION.
INVISIBILITY GLUE IN OLD CARTOONS.

DRUNK ONLINE PURCHASES.
SURPRISE VACATIONS.
BEING REBORN THROUGH INTIMACY.
BEING DESTROYED BY A GREAT POEM.

TALKING TO STRANGERS.
TAKING CANDY FROM STRANGERS.
TAKING UNKNOWN SUBSTANCES WITH STRANGERS.
CLASSICAL MUSIC PLAYING OVER VIOLENCE SCENES.
TAKING A SHIT AFTER DRINKING COFFEE.
TURNING ALL THE CRUCIFIXES UPSIDE-DOWN.
JUXTAPOSITION.
GIVING THINGS AWAY SPONTANEOUSLY.

BUYING CLOTHING OFF RANDOM PEOPLE VS SHOPPING.
BEING PROVEN WRONG WITH HARD PROOF.
ACTUALLY CHANGING YOUR MIND (ABOUT ANYTHING).
WHEN PEOPLE DANCE LIKE LUNATICS.

DAYDREAMS THAT BECOME REALITY.
WHEN WOMAN DRINK ME UNDER THE TABLE.
WHEN EXTREMELY OLD PEOPLE LAUGH HYSTERICALLY.
WHEN I CAN'T REFUSE AN OFFER.

MAKING ART IN OBSCURE MOMENTS AND PLACES.
LEARNING ABOUT NEW OR EXOTIC ANIMALS —
IMAGINARY CREATURES INCLUDED.
WHEN A BEAUTIFUL WOMAN FARTS OBSCENELY.

ENDING THINGS JUST BECAUSE.

SACCHARINE SACRILEGE

We are divinely drunk lovers
of exquisite vice and spontaneous virtue,
breaking down the old worlds
and crafting new worlds from their bones.

We stand atop a mountain of skulls
from all our conquered demons.
Champions of a dissolving hell.
A nightmare tamed and bottled.

Her excess is intoxicating.
mighty is femininity unbound.
Her beauty is enthralling.
I weep even at her reflection.

She makes me laugh until madness,
dragging my love past all sadness.
I pluck the stars from the sky
and place them in her undying eyes.

We sleep atop a mountain of calcium dust.
The remains of extinct angels.
Victorious in vanquishing heaven,
the illusion dispelled and expired.

Her devotion is profound.
extinguishing the flames of fear,
Her tranquility is pristine,
or at least until the next hunt begins.

DELIBERATE EXTINCTION

I RECALL
IT WAS POURING RAIN THAT DAY
BUT IN MY MIND
IT WAS THE TEARS OF A FORGOTTEN ANGEL
FALLING DOWN
FROM A HOLLOW SKY.

IT MIGHT AS WELL
HAVE BEEN THE LAST DAY ON EARTH,
BOTH OF US
LAUGHING MANIACALLY
AT HOW FULL
OUR HEARTS HAD BECOME.

WE MADE LOVE
AS IF WE INTENDED TO SHATTER
EACH OTHER'S BONES,
AND JUST MAYBE
SOMEHOW
WE DID.

JUST TO LEAVE A MARK
UPON OUR SOULS,
JUST TO WITNESS
AN END TO OUR PAST,
IT WAS SWEET EXTINCTION
ONE WORTH HOLDING ON TO.

KEEP YOUR DE-COMPOSURE

A million deaths gather here today
into a fistful of deep black soil.

Molecules fuse from universal disorder
into precious and vital nutrition.

A sea of oblivion has found
a ship of spontaneous purpose.

All emaciated meaning
now plump with the flesh of future.

With the simple act of planting a seed
we transform death back into life.

By decomposing we liberate potential
held like so much light in a jar.

Paradise is born
from the ashes of angels.

Hell has always been
denying water to thy garden.

Dirt is but a mass grave from which
everything beautiful shall bloom.

MAYFLIES

SITTING HERE SPLIT LIKE THE ATOM
DIVIDED AND BLOWN APART,
SO HOPELESSLY IN LOVE
AS INNER MAGNETS WHIRL
AND TWIRL ROUND A WANDERING CORE,
FREEDOM DISSOLVES THE CRAVINGS.
BROKEN AND BEAUTIFUL,
DERANGED AND DELIGHTED.

MOLECULAR VISIONS SCREAM AND EXPIRE.
MAYFLIES OF THE MIND
RIDING ELECTRIC WAVES,
CASHING DROWNING DEPTHS.
IMAGES IMAGINING THEMSELVES
PROCREATING ASEXUAL INFINITUDES,
CONSUME OR BE CONSUMED
MERGE OR BE VANQUISHED.

COLD SEASON THAWING RAPIDLY,
RELEASES HIBERNATING VERSES,
THE EARTH AND ITS EVOLVING WARDROBE.
WE ALL HAVE A DATE WITH A DYING STAR.
HESITATION MARKS THE UNMOVED,
MASTURBATION AND BOOZE
WAITING FOR SOMETHING BIG
EDGING BACK TRANSCENDENCE.

SOFT MACHINES LOST IN DREAMS.
DAYS OF LABOR NIGHTS OF DECAY
MADNESS IS THE LOCOMOTION
OF LINGUISTIC LIBERATION.
LIMBO IS EXPANDING
AS HEAVEN AND HELL VANISH
BOHEMIAN BOREDOM UNVEILS
QUEUE THE ESSENCE OF TRAGIC LAUGHTER.

POISON IS THE MEDICINE

A string of bleeding hearts
flicker like old Christmas lights
in a dark deserted alley.

A ghostly radiance
illuminates utter solitude
with a pale invitation.

The harp of discontent
plays melodies to the lost,
unmatched by siren or angel.

Vivid petals drip down
offering delicate poison
and violent love.

A constant seduction
to something once precious
and now abandoned.

R.I.P. (REST IN POWDER)

Sing me an epic
and bring me home.
Smash me against
the unforgiving rocks
and leave my heart at sea.

Siren bind me to my destiny
out past the sun's reach,
into the dens of strange beasts
make me a greater creature
refashion the man I was.

Play with my soul
like a child's toy.
Make a world from my misery
and then toss me to the wolves
so that I may feed the future.

Leave my effigies
scatted in the ash
break apart my molecules
and disperse them like dust,
too small to re-collect,
too many to ever count.

Hold my visions
within eternal flame.
Burn away my memories
from my white-hot skull.
Imprint every bit of me.
Seal me in pow(d)er.
Disembowel me
like a sacrificial lamb.
Take the meat from me
and make me holy.
Remind us that blood is art.

MAKE BELIEVE

There is no such thing as...
a vacation.
a way out.
total peace.
redemption.
purity.
comprehending the infinite
dead space.

There is no such thing as...
adults.
or enlightenment.
that persists.

Humans are addicted...
to false patterns.
mental constructs.
simplifying things.
the idea of absolutes.
to fear.
stress.
and gossip.

Humans are addicted...
to chemicals galore
and the perpetual.

We are liars
who lie to ourselves.
we lie in such a way
that the lie remains hidden.

Liars lying
to each other
just to keep the lie
alive.

GOSSAMER DREAM

False prophets command lies
in their castles of paranoia and illusion.
The stench of arrogance
fills our air and poisons the wells.

The rich swim in filthy imaginations,
tripping like cult leaders on immortalities,
Swallowing everything just to sustain consumption,
Harvesting the very heart of the earth.

Nihilistic youth suck out the marrow of existence.
posthumous fame on MeTube. Live Stream
Ignorance like a fetid and expanding swamp
pulling its surroundings down into its muck.

Yet in all of this – A moment, a wave, a way
Weaving like sunlight through a dark meadow
Wrapped around this – A pulse, a crystal finite, a chance
Dissolving all of time into pure experience.

Honest men carrying out simple lives
in their homes of love and lust.
The silent screams of nothing special
echo down and through the city streets

The destitute float on gossamer dreams
getting high off nothing but slim possibilities
Slipping further down just to stay alive
bleeding out pride to feed hope's machine.

Spoiled children spitting out all their lessons
that which cannot be critiqued is invincible to evolution.
War of absentia brings its casualties to the stagnant mind
dragging down the average of all our potential.

Yet in all of this – A moment, a wave, a way
Weaving like sunlight into a dark meadow
Wrapped around this – A pulse, a crystal finite, a chance
Dissolving all of time into pure experience.

The wicked shall forever remain wicked
but the righteous will still be dancing like far away stars.
The fire of evil cannot be quenched,
yet the heroes shall still bring water from hidden places.

SAVAGE SURPLUS

No level of intoxication
could numb his heart
thinking of everything, always
from now and back to the start.

It wasn't because he was broken
but rather filled to the brim
spewing from every minute crack
and never letting the light dim.

He loved so intensely
that it paralyzed his tongue,
overtook by elite allure
every day since he was young.

Years and tears of joy
consuming all his chances,
time bursting forth
washing away all his romances.

Life was wicked to his lot
giving him more than his hands could carry,
Yet to the edge of the Earth
he held his burden to bury.

When he arrived
he tumbled over the brink,
his abundance cast like a bottle
into life's boundless sea.

AUTUMN TWILIGHT

This land is shedding its skin
to make room for it's dark twin.
Colors scream until they're gone
then burn slow into golden dawn.

We sit deathly still in silent motif,
holding on like the last quivering leaf.
Animals desperate for radiant sunlight.
Earth drains into surrendering white.

The world snake dies in plain sight
as sly foxes watch from buried might.
A falcon descends for one last meal
machine winding down with hollow squeal.

We walk through the long cold night
holding each-others dreams alight.
Gripping our shaking memories
rationing our immaculate reveries.

tomorrow's constant

In each delicate kiss
lies a cloaked dagger.
With every day of bliss
comes the doom to balance.

Fascination grips
the mind of every prisoner
at just how much the jailor
enjoys their suffering.

To see the world in infinite colors.
to know the touch of immaculate skin.
to taste of ripe forbidden fruits
is to simultaneously invite great sadness.

Weaved within our grand capacities
are sinister truths.
Sewn up in all our vast unknowns
is an agonizing constant.

We just cross our fingers and hope for the best.
we pray to silent gods with alcoholic breath.
we put ourselves down on beds of uncertainty
and wait for the medication to kick in.

Expecting in the morning
for the world to have changed.

STILL BURNING OFFERING

Don't be a fool!
you must seize your chance.
Follow the call
that screams beneath your ribs.

Invite the love within –
constantly
Accept the humility –
completely.

Your makeup
hasn't tricked anyone,
she was already laughing
you silly clown.

Give in –
to the sudden trance
Surrender –
to the wicked dance

Her smile is the cure
for all your sadness,
now kiss her as if
the world depended upon it.

Let go –
before you go numb
For tomorrow –
may never come.

A beautiful window
has opened up like a tear
in your dark little room –
removing years of stagnant air.

BREATHE YOUNG MAN –
TAKE HER IN LIKE A PRIZE
SHE IS NO ILLUSION –
NOR A TRICK UPON YOUR EYES.

JUST TREAT HER RIGHT
LET HER BE YOUR SCARLET ON SCREEN,
IT'S EASY YOU SHALL SEE.
SHE'S DEATH AND YOUR JAMES DEAN.

ALLOW HER SPELLS –
TO ENCHANT YOU
LET HER INCANTATIONS –
CONSUME YOU.

YOU'RE FAR TOO WEAK TO RESIST
A DREAM THIS EXQUISITE.
MAN IS ONLY AS GOOD
AS THE WOMAN HE IS OFFERED.

ASHES TO BALANCE

POETRY PULLED
FROM THE ASHES,
WORDS OF LOVE
IN TIMES OF CHAOS.

A WHISPER
OF COMPASSION
IN A SILENT
DEPRESSION.

A SMILE ON THE FACE
OF DEATH,
BLISS BLOOMING
OUT OF DESTRUCTION.

SUSTENANCE FOUND
FROM A COLD CARCASS,
THE GREATEST LOVE
BORN FROM HEARTBREAK.

TRUE STRENGTH
FROM PAST PAIN,
DIGNITY
FOLLOWING DISGRACE.

SHEDDING BLOOD
IN ORDER TO HEAL,
SCARS TRADED
FOR WARM MEMORIES.

HANDS THAT HOLD
THE FRAGILE BIRD,
HANDS THAT REMEMBER
DRAINING LIFE.

LIPS THAT KISS
SO DEARLY,
LIPS THAT HAVE LIED
SO PURELY.

MINDS THAT CAPTURE
IMAGINATION,
MINDS THAT IMPRISON
SORROW.

EXTREME WONDER
TIED TO SUBLIME FEAR,
CONSCIOUSNESS TEETERS
BETWEEN AWE AND DREAD.

MOMENTS BURIED
IN TIME'S VAST FABRIC,
MOMENTS SEALED
IN FATE'S BOOK.

A VIBRANT POPPY
SPROUTING IN THE DESERT SAND.
THE PERSISTENT WEED
THAT BURST THROUGH CONCRETE.

A STEADY MACHINE
THAT MANUFACTURES BEAUTY.
A RELENTLESS MACHINE
THAT CORRUPTS ITSELF.

THE END OF SUFFERING
IS THE END OF DISCOVERY.
A GLASS NEARLY FULL
BUT WITH THE VITAL ESSENCE ABSENT.

A MASTERPIECE INCINERATED
IN ORDER TO WARM OUR SOULS.

GOBELKLI TEPE

There's no poetry left
in these immortalities.

The lords of dissonance
have given birth
to endless Frankenstein's.

The harder we hold on
the less we understand.

Submerged in
an ever-changing river.

We cannot hope to grasp
what it means to be
the rushing waters.

Pyramids stacked
upon the ruins
of ever more ancient sites.

The open hand of man
begging for something to hold.

We are no longer
what we thought we were.

Subconscious lacunas
lead the way
to terra incognitos.

Keeping our true potential captive
Omnipotent and tongue-less.

Nature no longer finds us interesting.
The blinking of an all-seeing eye.

We cannot kill
that which we cannot name.

PESSIMISTIC SURVIVAL

Sifting through the ashes of paradise
for a bit of what remains.

Searching for cerulean moments
in seas of crimson red.

Neuronal electric,
Mental magnetic.

The slow alchemy
of internal fire.

Tiny doorways open in pitch blackness
but they remain too far away.

Tiny eclipses glitch across
the illuminated full moon.

I am just another ape
captured by the firefly's light.

The cliff always comes sooner
than my understanding of the fall.

ORIGIN STORY

My heart is pregnant
with an immaculate beast.
It begs to be born
and yearns to be free,
But first I must tell you
how it came to be.

It was conceived in a hospital
filled with sick children.
Some were friends that died before bedtime,
others just didn't have the right enzyme.
Surrounded by tubes and machines
sharp needles and death scenes,
collecting scars of every kind
even some just inside the mind.

It understands relentless rain
and the permanence of pain.

It never begged for sympathy
from tough or troubled times,
for a ghost that fathered
or rarely bothered.
One who punctuated timelines
and left stains like cheap wines.
Cigarette ashes in pop-cans
and booze-soaked hands.

This beast grows from a deeper truth
and away from the insanity of youth.

It was incubated by the tragedy
and the ruins of paradise
Fortified down in the meadow.

WHERE STRANGE FRUIT GROW
AND THE WILDFLOWERS STILL BURN,
WHERE THE BURIED SHALL NEVER RETURN.
LOVE UNREQUITED CAN DERANGE
BUT FROM THIS COMES HONEST CHANGE.

WITH HARSH WINDS AND COMPETITIVE SOIL
THE SEEDLING THRIVES AS IT'S FORCED TO TOIL.

BUT ALAS THESE TALES ARE STILLBIRTHS
THAT HAVE LONG AGO ESCAPED THEIR CAVITIES.
THEY NOW BLESS THE HALLOWED GROUND OF THE PAST
AND INTO THAT ANCIENT DARKNESS THEY ARE NOW CAST.
SUNK HAPPILY INTO PURE OBSCURITY,
MAKING ROOM FOR CONFIDENT SECURITY.
A DESIGNER CREATURE IS NOW FULLY FORMED
FROM HARDSHIPS AND TRIALS TRANSFORMED.

A BEAUTIFUL MONSTER IS BORN INTO THIS WORLD
FROM DESTRUCTION INTO SHEAR GRATITUDE IT IS HURLED.

invited trap

It's all so easy
once you find yourself
captured by
the right trap.

It becomes
a simple surrender
when eager lips
greet an aching chest.

The games
of the world
dissolve.

The carrots
upon their sticks
vanish.

Nothing left to chase –
fear just
unravels.

What is left
when your heart gives in?
All is but a dream
come to life.

What more
could one man ask for?
Flawless love
made flesh.

My heart swells up
like a child's smile
on Halloween night

STILL DRESSED UP
AS MY FAVORITE
CARTOON CHARACTER.

LYING IN A PILE
OF SACCHARINE BLISS,
SEALED WITH A KISS.

SERUM

I milk the venom
from every snake
I can find.

I pull the trigger
on every gun
every time.

I weave my moments
and twist them
into space-time.

My mind is screaming
a strange song
in chaos rhyme.

FORGIVE OR FORGET

Lust is expanding disorder.
Love is an indivisible atom.

Lust is a kind of slow death.
Love is the flower upon its grave.

Lust is an endless craving.
Love is a growing satiation.

Lust takes more than it needs.
Love gives more than you can handle.

Lust is a penny at the bottom of a wishing well.
Love is the vast fountain they lie in.

Lust will never forget.
Love can only forgive.

EARTHLY DELIGHTS

I AM
A SHAPESHIFTER
WHO IS RUNNING
RUN OUT OF SHAPES.

I AM
A CHAMELEON
WHO HAS FORGOTTEN
HIS TRUE COLORS.

I AM
A UNIVERSE
THAT HAS NO MORE
SPACE TO EXPAND.

I DISSOLVE
THE SELF
TO WITNESS
BEFORE MY BIRTH.

I EXTINGUISH
MY SOUL
INTO EACH NEW FLAME
THAT ARRIVES.

I WILL DIE
ON THE SPEAR OF LOVE
JUST TO LEAVE
A BODY BEHIND.

I WILL BURN
FOREVER
JUST TO UNDERSTAND
YOUR KIND.

There is always
one more
charming devil
with the deal of a lifetime.

There is always
one more
fallen angel
with scars and a story.

I will never
understand
the calculus
of paradise.

A plentiful life
traded
for a kingdom
of clouds.

BOTTOMLESS CUP

I sip my wine of plenty
and laugh at every thought
for my heart is over-ripe
at what this world has brought.

The hunt of the Black Dog
has long ago ended
in an immaculate kill
the feast of the splendid.

I stand atop a carcass
of all that was meek
soaked in blood like holy water
veiling the weak.

This love is a weapon
tempered under a blazing sun.
This love is a whore
purified like a born-again nun.

This love is a lesson
sharpened by pain.
This love is a victory
atop all it has slain.

I sip from my bottomless cup
and laugh at time's dooming,
for once again —
the wasteland is blooming.

"Mr. Morrow writes of worlds where inner demons, ghosts, and ghouls are real. His work reveals a dark purity that reminds us of the terror and the pleasure of being alive. Each word carries a weight which balances his poems, but can also make them so askew that the reader is left feeling overwhelmed by the staggering truth/untruth. His poems are about the person you see in your mind's eye when you look in the mirror, not the person that others know you as, but your true self...the one that scares you, the one that comforts you, the one that is capable of giving birth to entirely new worlds. It's within these worlds where savages run free, a drop of her sweat makes you immortal, and that damn stain won't come out. Contained in these works is the beauty of living, the brutality of living, and the inevitability of the end of living."

– Todd Nichols –

"WE HAVE NOT EVEN TO RISK THE ADVENTURE ALONE, FOR THE HEROES OF ALL TIME HAVE GONE BEFORE US. THE LABYRINTH IS THOROUGHLY KNOWN; WE HAVE ONLY TO FOLLOW THE THREAD OF THE HERO PATH. AND WHERE WE HAD THOUGHT TO FIND AN ABOMINATION, WE SHALL FIND A GOD. AND WHERE WE HAD THOUGHT TO SLAY ANOTHER, WE SHALL SLAY OURSELVES. AND WHERE WE HAD THOUGHT TO TRAVEL OUTWARD, WE SHALL COME TO THE CENTER OF OUR OWN EXISTENCE. AND WHERE WE HAD THOUGHT TO BE ALONE, WE SHALL BE WITH ALL THE WORLD"
- JOSEPH CAMPBELL -

"NOTHING RETAINS ITS FORM; NEW SHAPES FROM OLD. NATURE, THE GREAT INVENTOR, CEASELESSLY CONTRIVES. IN ALL CREATION, BE ASSURED, THERE IS NO DEATH - NO DEATH, BUT ONLY CHANGE AND INNOVATION; WHAT WE MEN CALL BIRTH IS BUT A DIFFERENT NEW BEGINNING; DEATH IS BUT TO CEASE TO BE THE SAME. PERHAPS THIS MAY HAVE MOVED TO THAT, AND THAT TO THIS, YET STILL THE SUM OF THINGS REMAINS THE SAME"
- OVID -

"BECAUSE THE WORLD IS SO FULL OF DEATH AND HORROR, I TRY AGAIN AND AGAIN TO CONSOLE MY HEART AND PICK THE FLOWERS THAT GROW IN THE MIDST OF HELL."
- HERMANN HESSE -

.

www.ingramcontent.com/pod-product-compliance
Lightning Source LLC
Chambersburg PA
CBHW071853090426
42811CB00004B/594